DISCOVERING WORLD CULTURES

Crabtree Publishing Company

PMB 16A, 350 Fifth Avenue
Suite 3308
New York, NY 10118

612 Welland Avenue
St. Catharines, Ontario
L2M 5V6

Created by McRae Books Srl
© McRae Books Srl 2001

Cataloging in Publication Data

MacDonald, Fiona, 1950-
  Homes / text by Fiona MacDonald ; illustrations by Antonella
Pastorelli, Ivan Stalio, Paola Ravaglia.
    p. cm. -- (Discovering world cultures)
  Includes index.
  ISBN 0-7787-0237-5 (RLB) -- ISBN 0-7787-0247-2 (pbk.)
    1. Dwellings--Juvenile literature. [1. Dwellings.]   I.
Pastorelli, Antonella, ill. II. Stalio, Ivan, ill. III. Ravaglia, Paola,
ill. IV. Title. V. Series.
  GT172 .M67 2001
  392.3'6--dc21
                                              00-069355
                                                 LC

Co-ordinating Editor: Ellen Rodger
Production Co-ordinator: Rosie Gowsell
McRae Books Srl
Editors: Holly Willis, Anne McRae
Illustrations: Daniela Astone, Lorenzo Cecchi, Matteo Chesi, Gian Paolo Faleschini, Jean-Marie Guillou,
Andrea Ricciardi di Gaudesi, Paola Ravaglia, Studio Stalio (Alessandro Cantucci, Fabiano Fabbrucci, Andrea Morandi, Ivan Stalio),
Design: Marco Nardi, Adriano Nardi, Laura Ottina

Color separations: Litocolor, Florence, Italy
1234567890   Printed and bound in Italy by Nuova G.E.P.   0987654321

HOMES

Text by Fiona MacDonald

Illustrations by Daniela Astone, Antonella Pastorelli,
Studio Stalio, Paola Ravaglia

Crabtree
www.crabtreebooks.com

List of Contents

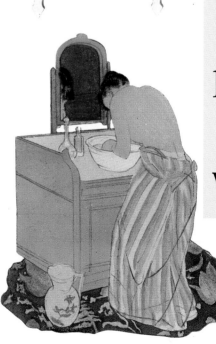

On stilts

In countries where there are heavy rains and frequent floods, people build their houses high above ground. In Cambodia, many houses like this, in the Mekong River Delta region, are built on tall wooden stilts. The people who live there reach them by boat.

This Cambodian house withstood massive floods in 1991.

Can be portable

Traditionally, many peoples of Central Asia were nomadic, moving from place to place to find fresh **pasture** for their animals. They lived in portable tent-like homes, called *yurts*, made of thick felt cloth.

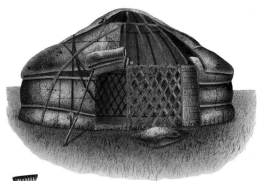

This Mongolian yurt has a framework of collapsible wooden poles.

Homes around the world

People all over the world build shelters to live in. The shelters, or homes they live in are not all the same. They vary in shape and size. People's houses also reflect the environment they live in. Houses for cold climates need to be different from houses where the weather is hot. Wealthy people live in houses very different from poor peoples' homes. Religious and cultural beliefs also influence house design.

On the water

Kashmir, a disputed territory between India and Pakistan, is a land of mountains and lakes. There is very little land for building. So people living in crowded towns build houseboats, such as these dongas. They are set up along the shores of Dal Lake in the Indian city of Srinagar.

For shepherds

In Europe, shepherds used to live in wagons or caravans while looking after their flocks in remote pastures. Made of brightly-painted wood, the wagons had high arched roofs, to create more space inside. They were heated by wood stoves, and pulled by horses or steam-powered engines.

This man stands in the doorway of an old wagon he has restored to use as a weekend home.

Dongas (left) are built of wood. Their name comes from the wooden shingles, or small tiles, used to make their roofs.

The steep sloping roofs of the trulli houses (below) are designed so that rainwater will run off and collect in underground cisterns, or storage tanks, for later use.

Made for the heat

In Italy, the weather is often hot and very dry. These trulli houses, in traditional beehive shape, are built with thick stone walls that keep the houses cool inside. The walls are also whitewashed, to reflect or turn away as much of the sun's heat as possible.

The steep sloping roof of this minka (below) lets heavy rainfall run off quickly, so that it does not soak in and ruin the thatch.

In the trees

In Irian Jaya, Indonesia, the Kombai and Korowai people build houses high in rainforest trees. The houses are sometimes 164 feet (50 meters) above ground. Traditionally, this is to keep families safe from evil spirits, who do not like to climb that high.

Each treehouse (right) is reached by a swaying rope-ladder, which can be pulled up when enemies or dangerous wild animals approach. Small children and favorite hunting dogs are carried up the ladder by adults at night.

Safe from storms

This *minka*, or traditional farmhouse, in Japan is built of materials from the surrounding countryside: pinewood and rice-straw **thatch**. Inside, the walls are made of paper, also produced from rice-straw. The *minka's* wooden beams are put together in a way that allows them to move slightly during earthquakes and violent storms.

With light

In the 1700s and 1800s, there was an increase in the goods traded long-distance by sea. To protect ship cargos, many lighthouses were built around dangerous coasts. Their flashing lanterns warned sailors of rocks. Lighthouse-keepers lived in cottages close by. They had to be on duty day and night to make sure that the lighthouse lanterns kept burning brightly.

This lighthouse (below), with its lighthouse keeper's cottage, is at Cape Neddick on the coast of Maine, USA.

This farm room (left) is for storing millet, an edible grain. Its walls are made of brushwood, covered in mud and dung, and its roof is made of dried-grass thatch.

Used as storehouses

In Rajastan, northwest India, farming families build houses containing several separate rooms arranged around a courtyard and surrounded by a strong fence. Each room has a separate function. Some rooms are for sleeping, others are for entertaining visitors, and some are for storing grain. The courtyard also contains a **shrine**, where prayers are said.

This 1810 house in Mississippi, was the home of Confederate President Jefferson Davis during the American Civil War.

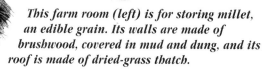

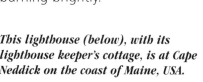

Away from the cities

As cities in Europe and North America grew larger, dirtier, and noisier during the 19th century, families who could afford to move built newer, larger homes. They moved to the countryside or to residential districts on the outskirts of big towns, called suburbs.

Wood and stone

Stone is the strongest, longest-lasting building material, but it is very heavy, and needs a lot of support. This building in central India has a roof made from thick slabs of stone. They are held up by pillars of wood.

Timber!

Many different kinds of trees are used to provide lumber for building. Fast-growing **softwoods**, such as spruce and pine, are cheap and plentiful. They must be treated with chemical preservatives, or they will rot. Slow-growing tropical **hardwoods**, such as teak, are expensive but much stronger. Sadly, the Asian rainforests where they grow have been cut down by logging companies, so that many hardwood trees are now almost wiped out. Some ancient softwood forests in North America are also in danger.

Huge logs cut from forest trees are transported by road and river to lumber yards and building sites.

Building materials

Today, many buildings are constructed from materials made in factories: strong steel **girders**, slabs of concrete, and sheets of tinted glass. Modern **architects** choose materials that are in fashion or are inspired by recent developments in engineering. But in the past, things were very different. Builders had to use the materials they found locally. It was too difficult, and expensive, to transport wood, clay, or stone long distances by sea or overland. Local materials had a great influence on traditional building styles. Often, they were only suitable for buildings of certain shapes or sizes. Traditional building skills were handed on from **generation** to generation, so that local builders copied earlier designs with very few changes.

Buildings made of wood and straw attract insects. If left to breed, they can cause serious damage. The inside of this building is usually whitewashed, for decoration and to keep insects away.

Brickmaking

Bricks are one of the oldest building materials. There are two main kinds of brick, sun-dried and fired. Sun-dried bricks are made by leaving blocks of mud in the hot sun to dry. Fired bricks are baked at high temperatures in an oven called a kiln.

In India, bamboo buildings are constructed by a special caste, or group, of workers. They pass skills down through their families.

Tree-trunk supports

This church (above) in Morrope, Brazil, dates from around 1580, but was made using techniques that are thousands of years old. Strong trunks of the algarrobo tree were shaped to create pillars and **rafters**. The roof is made of strips of **cane**.

Bamboo and thatch

Building stone is always expensive, and is not easily found in many areas. A wide variety of plants are used to provide building materials instead. This house, in India, has walls made of **bamboo** poles and a roof made with rice-straw. Bamboo is light and flexible, but will rot if it gets too wet.

Ice houses

In the Arctic, traditional dome-shaped houses called *iglus* are made of blocks of compressed snow and ice. Their thick walls provide good insulation, keeping the people inside warm. *Iglus* are not designed for long-term living. Usually, they are built as temporary shelter on hunting or fishing trips.

Building an iglu (above). The walls are constructed as a spiral, with a wide circle at ground level and a circular block at the top.

Hunting shelters of African rainforest peoples were made from branches and leaves.

Adobe

Pueblos are the **communal** homes of Native American people in New Mexico. They are built of *adobe,* a local clay which is formed into bricks. Pueblos join small family houses together in terraces, reached by ladders and walkways across flat roofs.

This adobe Pueblo is in Taos, New Mexico. Its small windows stop bright desert sunlight from entering the rooms inside.

Branches and leaves

Traditionally, rainforest peoples of western and central Africa built hunting shelters out of flexible branches woven into a dome shape. They covered them with layers of tough, waterproof, forest leaves that protected the hunters from heavy rain.

Dry-grass thatch

In West Africa, traditional homes are built of mud-brick or concrete blocks, with roofs made from bundles of dried grass tied to wooden rafters. If the thatch is thick, and steeply sloped, it stays waterproof for years.

Skin tents

Native American peoples living in the Great Plains region of North America built tipis, or tents, for shelter. Tipis were made of buffalo skins, stitched together and rubbed with fat to make them waterproof. They were stretched over long wooden poles and had an opening at the top to allow smoke from the fire inside to escape. The floors of tipis were covered with blankets and rugs.

Tipis were easy to take down and pack away.

Carpenters, like the one in this illustration, made timber frames for houses in Europe during the Middle Ages. They cut and shaped each wooden beam and rafter, then fitted them together, and covered them with woven twigs mixed in clay. Some timber-framed houses in Europe are over 500 years old.

Using tools

Until the late 19th century, buildings were made by hand. Saws were used for cutting large lengths of wood, hammers and mallets for knocking nails and wooden pegs into lumber. Chisels and planes were used for trimming and shaping wooden beams, doors, and window frames.

In prehistoric times

Some of the earliest homes built were simple shelters made under outcrops of rock. Inside, early humans made a **hearth**, surrounded by stones and straw beds. There was space for cooking, working, and sleeping by the fire.

Rock shelters (left) were made from tree branches, covered with a canopy of animal skins held in place by ropes made from plant fibers.

Made from bones

Around 16,000 B.C., hunter-gatherers in the Ukraine built circular huts of mammoth bones. They found the bones at a mammoth "graveyard," a place where mammoths went to die, and used them to make a framework for walls and roofs. They covered the bones with **turf** and with animal hides.

Homes through history

Ever since people first lived together in families, their basic needs have been the same. They wanted shelter from wind, rain, and sometimes sun. They needed a fire to provide heat and for cooking, somewhere safe and comfortable to sleep, and a place to hide from enemies or wild animals. Ancient peoples made houses from building materials that were available nearby. Building styles and materials changed over time as people became more skilled.

These village houses, made of wood and straw thatch, were built by farmers in Banpo, China, around 6,000 B.C.

In Bible lands

This large house (left) was built in **Palestine** around the 1st century A.D. At that time, most people lived in villages and made a living from farming or trading. Unlike prehistoric homes (above), this house has separate rooms for cooking, eating, sleeping, and washing. It was made of sun-dried mud brick, covered with a layer of plaster. Thick walls helped keep it cool in summer and warm in winter. Privacy was preserved by small windows and an enclosed inner courtyard.

This house belonged to a wealthy Roman. It is large and even has room for a shop.

For a rich Roman

In ancient Rome, wealthy people lived in large, beautiful homes. The homes were decorated with statues and artwork. **Roman** houses were usually arranged around courtyards, sometimes with gardens and pools.

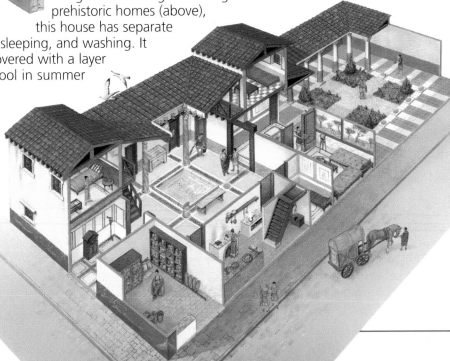

For an emperor

This **mosaic** shows the palace built for emperor Theodoric the Great, who ruled Italy, Sicily, and parts of Germany and Yugoslavia from 471–526 A.D. It shows the entrance to the palace and the grand halls, with high arched windows and curtains.

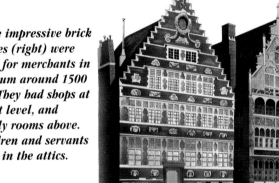

Himeji castle, in Japan, was built for a powerful samurai family around 1600. Samurai were noble warriors.

During the Renaissance

Many fine homes were built during the **Renaissance**; a time of great achievements in art and learning in Europe, from 1400 to 1600. Families who had grown rich through trade, exploration, or war, paid for many stylish new houses, as well as for works of art.

In Japan

Japanese castles (right) were built of wood and plaster on top of a strong stone base. Their graceful curved roofs were made of clay tiles. They were built for defense and to display the owners' wealth, status, and artistic good taste.

This early Renaissance painting by Jan van Eyck is called The Arnolfini Marriage. *It shows the inside of a wealthy merchant's house. The bed was draped with red velvet, a valuable material for the time. There is an expensive rug on the floor and a chandelier.*

These impressive brick houses (right) were built for merchants in Belgium around 1500 A.D. They had shops at street level, and family rooms above. Children and servants slept in the attics.

Inspired by the past

From Renaissance times until today, many builders and architects have copied ancient Greek and Roman designs. They admired the elegance and style of ancient buildings. Builders have also copied many Greek and Roman decorative features in smaller homes, such as tall columns at doorways, and patterns based on scrolls, zigzags, and leaves.

The Villa Rotunda (left), in Italy, was designed by architect Andrea Palladio in the 1500s. It is based on Greek designs, and is decorated with Greek-style statues.

Using modern design

The Schroeder house in Utrecht, Netherlands, (below) was designed by Gerrit Rietveld in 1924. In the early 20th century, there was a revolution in architectural ideas. Architects began to believe that "form should follow function," which means that the appearance of each building should be based on how it is used and not on patterns added for decoration. They designed new, modern buildings, with block-like shapes and plain exteriors.

The design of this 19th century wooden house in New York, was based on ancient Greek architecture.

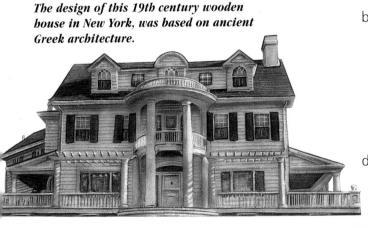

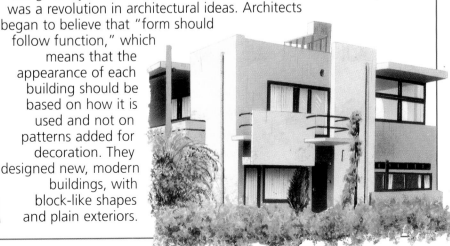

Homes for rich...

This villa, or country house, was built around 1480 A.D. for the very wealthy Medici family, who made their fortune as bankers in the city of Florence, Italy. The villa was used as a summer residence; a cool, quiet escape from the city's noise and dirt.

.... and poor

In many countries, poor people live in makeshift homes built of old planks of wood and corrugated iron, gathered from garbage dumps. They have no running water, no electricity, and no backyards where their children can play in safety. Behind them, high rise blocks of apartments provide homes for people who can afford to pay high rent.

Social differences

Wealthy people often own many large homes. Poor people sometimes have difficulty finding any home at all. For the wealthy, homes are status symbols, designed to impress others. All around the world, wealthy people have built large houses, with many more rooms than they need, as a sign of their money and power. At the same time, poor people survive as best as they can in homes made of inexpensive or available material, without clean running water or electricity.

Poor at the top...

During the 19th century, many big cities in Europe and North America grew very quickly as people moved to them in search of work. Tall buildings, with impressive **facades** were built in many of these cities to provide housing and working space for people. Low-paid workers and servants lived in small, cramped attic rooms at the top.

Rich in the middle...

Wealthy families lived in spacious apartments in the middle of each block. Their rooms had high ceilings, large windows, and balconies. They were at a safe distance from the noise and dirt of the street below, and from the damp, smoky feeling of the attics.

Shops on the street

At street level, big city buildings had space for several shops, with big glass windows where goods were often displayed. Their doors opened straight on to walkways. Shop owners and their families ate and slept in small dark rooms at the back of the shop.

Dispossessed

After European settlers arrived in North America, many Native American peoples were driven away from their lands. They were forced to travel long distances to make new homes on **reservations**. Reservation land was often poor, and unsuitable for hunting or farming, making it very difficult for native peoples to survive.

This illustration is of a Native American called Captain Joseph. He failed in his attempt to escape the U.S., and lead his people to Canada.

The president's home

In almost every country, all around the world, the **head of state** lives in a grand home, where he or she works and receives important visitors from other lands. The 100-room White House in Washington D.C. has been the official home of every American president and his family since 1800.

This American house (left) is built of clapboard, or overlapping planks of wood nailed on a strong wood frame. Lumber is plentiful in the eastern states of the U.S., and, for many years, it was a favorite building material.

This monk from the Middle Ages (below) is sitting at a desk in a special writing room, called a scriptorium. The light from the open window helps him to see his work clearly.

Suburban dream

For many North American middle-class families in the 20th century, the suburban dream meant owning a house outside the city center.

Inner city blues

In the late 20th century, many inner-city districts became run down and neglected, as residents and businesses moved to new suburbs. People who did not have the money to move away stayed in the crumbling inner-city.

Neglected inner-city districts, like this one in Philadelphia, are known as ghettos, a word originally used to describe an enclosed area in European towns where Jewish people were forced to live.

Separated

Members of religious communities from different **faiths** often choose to live shut away from the world, so that they can feel closer to God. Sometimes, they devote themselves to special tasks, such as hand copying the **Bible** or other religious texts.

Furniture

Houses provide shelter, but without furniture, they are not very comfortable to live in. People need somewhere to sleep, somewhere to sit, and somewhere to prepare food. All over the world, people have created furniture to meet these needs. They have used many different materials, and many different designs, depending on their wealth, lifestyle, and the local environment. Some furniture is plain and simple and some is very **elaborate**.

The Dutch artist Vincent van Gogh painted this bedroom in Arles, France in 1888. It contains simple furniture – a wooden bed and table, and two wooden chairs.

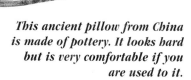

Daily life at home

A famous French architect once called houses "machines for living." He thought houses should be designed to make people's everyday lives as pleasant, comfortable, and convenient as possible. All around the world, people have built homes to meet their needs. People with large families need plenty of space in or around their homes, where their children can sleep and play. In cold climates, people need houses with good insulation and heating systems to keep their houses warm. People who entertain guests a lot look for houses with large living and dining rooms where they can relax and share meals.

This ancient pillow from China is made of pottery. It looks hard but is very comfortable if you are used to it.

Hammocks

Hammocks are beds made of fabric, rope, or netting. They are light, portable, and can be hung from posts or trees. Hammocks keep sleeping people safe above ground, out of reach of dangerous animals or insects. Unlike beds with thick mattresses, they are cool and airy, and do not collect moisture, or rot. This is especially important in hot, wet climates. Hammocks originated in South America, where they are still used by Native peoples today. When European sailors first arrived in the Caribbean in the 1500s, they liked the hammocks used by local people so much that they copied them for use below decks on their ships.

In Japan people traditionally sleep on Tatami mats made of woven grass. Tatami are thin and light, so it is easy to roll them up during the day. Then the room can be used for more than just sleeping.

A grandfather from the Yanomami people relaxes with his grandchild in a hammock made of plant fibers. The Yanomami live in the rainforest regions of Brazil and Venezuela, in South America.

Sleeping quarters

On average, people spend one third of their lives sleeping. Sleep is important for regenerating the body. All over the world, people sleep in different kinds of beds. Some people sleep on simple floor mats, while others use hammocks or woven beds on stands called charpoys. Bedrooms differ from culture to culture. In some cultures, the sleeping area of a house is also the living area during the day.

Dining rooms

Sharing a meal with family members or with invited guests is an important social occasion. Eating together creates close bonds. Hospitality is a social duty in many parts of the world. Where people eat is less important than the food offered, or the company at mealtime. Sometimes houses have separate dining rooms. Sometimes families gather around tables in their living areas to eat, while families in other countries share food from dishes placed on the ground.

An informal dinner at a country house in France, painted in the early 20th century. Wealthy families liked to entertain their guests in style. Here, the large mahogany table is covered with a white linen tablecloth and decorated with silver candlesticks and fresh flowers.

This French living room painted around 1880, is furnished in fashionable oriental style. Wealthy people relaxed in rooms like this one (below).

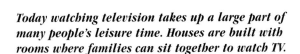

This Indian housewife (below) is cooking her family meal in an iron bowl over a fire in a clay pot. Her kitchen is a corner of one room, with a single shelf for storage jars. She has no running water, stove, freezer, or refrigerator.

Kitchens

Most homes have some kind of bedroom or living areas. In many countries and cultures, people do not have separate areas for preparing food. Food is sometimes stored in a pantry off of the main living area, and cooked on a central fire, also located near the main living area. Sometimes, meals are cooked in courtyards or out in the open air.

Living rooms

In large North American and European houses, where space can be easily divided and used for different purposes, bedrooms are the most private parts of the house. Only family members and trusted guests are invited there. Living rooms are considered less private, and are designed for relaxation and entertainment. Often, they are comfortably furnished with sofas, cushions, and carpets on the floor.

Working at home

During the 20th century, new inventions in **communications**, such as **faxes**, computers, and **modems**, made it possible for many people to work at home. This marked a great change from the way people worked in 19th century Europe and North America, when most wage earners left their homes to work in factories and offices.

Today watching television takes up a large part of many people's leisure time. Houses are built with rooms where families can sit together to watch TV.

Hung with pictures

Many people like to decorate the walls of their homes with paintings, posters, and photographs. This 19th century painting shows an elegant room in a palace in Naples, Italy. It is decorated with expensive and ornately framed oil paintings.

Carpets can be used as prayer mats or for receiving guests. This carpet from the Middle East is unique because it has been handwoven.

Walls and floors

Walls and floors divide one room from another and provide a level surface for walking, sitting, and sleeping. People in different lands decorate their walls and floors in many different ways. Sometimes walls and floors are painted and sometimes they are polished or stained. Often walls are covered with textiles, such as tapestries and hangings, while mats, rugs, and carpets are placed on the floors. Rugs and wall hangings bring color and texture to homes.

Covered with carpets and rugs

Carpets like this have often been used as status symbols. When they were first brought to Europe from Asia, during the late Middle Ages, they were too valuable to be put on floors, but were draped over tables, instead. Top quality carpets are still very valuable today.

Decorated with wall hangings

Wall hangings have been used all over the world to decorate rooms or to insulate against the cold. Different **embroidering** techniques and types of painting are used to decorate valuable cloth such as silk. Wall hangings often depict myths or religious stories and can be a way of recording and passing on ancient legends and stories.

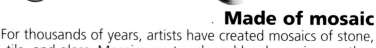

In Japan, floors are covered with tatami mats made of woven grass, which are also used for sitting and sleeping. Visitors take off their shoes, to keep the mats clean.

Made of mosaic

For thousands of years, artists have created mosaics of stone, tile, and glass. Mosaics are tough and hard-wearing, so they make ideal decorations for floors. Roman mosaic artists used to line pools and fountains with mosaics, to create special underwater effects.

Mosaics like this one, showing two roosters, often decorated the homes of wealthy ancient Romans.

The former bedroom of the Dalai lama, head of the Tibetan Buddhist religion, is richly decorated with wall hangings called tankas. These paintings show religious scenes and are used by Tibetan monks to help them meditate. They are beautifully mounted on silk backgrounds, like these ones behind the bed.

Painted on the outside

Traditionally, the Mangbetu people of central Africa, painted the outside of important buildings with red and black geometric designs.

In Poland, leaves and flowers painted on inside walls and on furniture (above) are symbols of life, hope, and joy.

This mosaic floor (left) was made during the 1700s to decorate a church on the Italian island of Anacapri. It shows the Bible story of Adam and Eve in the Garden of Eden. This mosaic is unusual, because it is made from large, square, painted tiles, rather than tiny pieces.

Tell stories

Mosaic floors are sometimes made in swirling or **geometric** patterns. They are also decorated with pictures that tell stories. In **Christian** churches, these are usually religious stories from the Bible.

This fresco was painted in the first century B.C. on the walls of a villa near Rome. It gives the illusion of being outside, by depicting a beautiful garden scene.

Keep evil away

In Tamil Nadu, southern India, women traditionally painted a *kolam* pattern outside their homes every day. It was made of rice flour mixed with water, and was a lucky charm, designed to keep evil spirits away. All the lines of the pattern meet so that evil can be caught.

Create illusions

Sometimes walls and ceilings are painted to look like the sky, with birds, stars, or clouds. They can show pictures of people or **saints** and can be decorated with geometric patterns, to complement designs on the floors. Frescoes are pictures that have been painted onto a wall or ceiling while the plaster is still wet. This helps to make the colors more vivid, and was popular during the Renaissance.

This mask keeps watch over the entrance to a temple in India.

Protect

Doors and gates are a barrier against danger. They stop unwanted things or people from entering a building. Traditionally, many doorways have been decorated with paintings or carvings of spirit-guardians to help protect the people inside.

The huge, open carved stone mouth (above) surrounds a window in the Zuccari Palace in Rome.

Doors and windows

Doors have great significance in many cultures. They mark an entrance and exit to a building. Every house needs at least one door, but not all doors look the same. Some doors are at ground level, while others are reached by steps or ladders. Some doors are trap doors, set into floors or ceilings and leading to attic or basement rooms. Big buildings, walls, and fences are guarded by strong doors called gates. Windows also form a barrier between people inside a house and the world outside. While doors are often solid, windows are **transparent**, letting in views and sunlight.

Let in light and air

Windows are designed to let light and air into buildings. They make rooms brighter and easier to work in. Today, windows are made of glass, but, until the 19th century, glass windows were too expensive for many ordinary people to use in their homes. Before then, windows were just holes in walls, covered by sheets of oiled cloth or wooden shutters.

In eastern Russia and Siberia, windows were traditionally decorated with carved wooden frames, called nalichniki. Nalichniki were carved by peasant farmers during the winter, when it was too cold to work outside.

Celebrate occasions

Guests entering a building for a special celebration, such as a wedding are often welcomed by the sight of decorations at doors and windows.

Bring peace and happiness

These painted wooden doors on a house in Gujarat, western India, are decorated with swastikas, a traditional Indian sign of good fortune. The name of the swastika design comes from the ancient word 'svasti', which means 'happiness'.

The doorway of this house in Bihar, eastern India, has been decorated with a pattern in rice flour mixed with water.

Tell Bible stories

Before the 1700s in Europe, many people could not read or write. To teach the Christian faith, churches were often decorated with stories from the Bible, told in pictures. Some pictures were painted on church walls, others were shown in windows of stained glass. Using the windows in this way let light in the church.

These huge gold and bronze gates mark the entrance to the Baptistery, where new Christians are baptized, in Florence, Italy. They are known as the Gates of Paradise.

This stained glass window was made for the cathedral in Bourges, France.

Keep out the cold

In the harsh mountain climate of Bolivia in South America, traditional homes are built without windows and with only one door. The door always faces away from the strong winds that blow across the high plateau lands where many Bolivian people live.

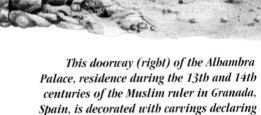

Welcome worshipers

Religious buildings belonging to many faiths often have large, impressive doorways. They remind worshipers that, by passing through them, they are entering a holy space and walking on holy ground. They should leave behind their everyday thoughts, and concentrate on their prayers.

Reflect customs

The Merina people of Madagascar believe that the northeast corner of a house is sacred. Food and valuables are placed there as offering to their ancestors. All the windows and doors in Merina houses traditionally face west, while the hearth faces south.

This doorway (right) of the Alhambra Palace, residence during the 13th and 14th centuries of the Muslim ruler in Granada, Spain, is decorated with carvings declaring God's greatness, and calling people to prayer.

Send religious messages

Islamic art is full of intricate patterns, designs, and writings. Traditional Islamic art does not depict living things such as people or animals because **Muslims** believe only Allah, or God, can create living things. Muslim artists decorate doorways with verses from the Muslim holy book, the *Qur'an*.

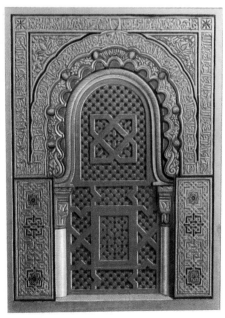

In wash-stands and tubs

Until the 20th century, many homes did not have indoor bathrooms. Even in wealthy, industrialized countries, people used wash stands, which were tables holding basins of water, or they bathed in wooden tubs. In wealthy homes, servants carried clean water to bedrooms every morning and took away dirty water after it was used.

This picture of a woman at a wash stand was made by American artist Mary Cassat in 1891.

This late 19th century photograph (right) shows two young Japanese women sharing a bath.

This painting by Dutch artist Adriaen van Jansz shows fish waiting to be washed at the water pump in a courtyard during the 17th century.

Water in the home

Water is essential for life. We need water for drinking, washing, cleaning, and for carrying away waste from our homes. Today, in many countries, people take clean water and good sewage systems for granted. Running water and sewage systems were introduced less than 150 years ago. Before that, water had to be carried to houses from rivers, wells, fountains, or open storage tanks. Toilets were just buckets, or holes in the ground. Even today, people in many countries live without reliable sewage systems or water supplies.

To keep clean

In many societies, people believed that "cleanliness was next to godliness." Keeping clean was important. Without modern piped water supplies and dish or clothes washers, this ideal of cleanliness took a lot of work. Heavy buckets of cold water had to be pumped up from wells outside, and carried indoors. Clothes, dishes, walls, and floors had to be washed by hand.

This Indian woman (above) pumps water from a community well located near her home. The well supplies water to many families in her village.

Or lack of water

Many homes and villages in the developing world still do not have reliable water supplies. Women and children spend hours every day collecting water from rivers and streams. To help them, international organizations raise money to work with local people to dig village wells.

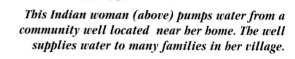

In bathrooms

By the late 19th century, wealthy peoples' homes had gas-fired boilers, to heat water for baths. This became possible because piped water systems were installed in big cities and towns around 1850. The first **mass-produced** flush toilets, manufactured by Thomas Crapper in London, also relied on piped water. They were connected to an underground network of pipes and sewers installed in towns and cities.

Rain is collected in reservoirs, and flows to waterworks. The water is filtered to remove dirt and bacteria. It is then disinfected and pumped to storage tanks, and sent through pipes to houses.

This illustration of a woman enjoying a warm bath, appeared in a book explaining how gas could be used to make homes more comfortable. The boiler that heated her bath water is in front of the tub.

This toilet was the latest technology in 1894. Water stored in the cistern, or overhead tank, washed waste away when the chain was pulled.

reservoir

storage tower

filter bed

settling tank

chlorine tank

pump

pipe to homes

For drinking

Clean drinking water has dramatically improved public health in developed countries in the past 150 years. Before then, water polluted by sewage, dirt, and chemicals was dangerous. Even today, dirty drinking water kills at least 25,000 people every day, worldwide. Many who die are young children who do not survive the diseases caused by bad water.

Used by appliances

Modern household appliances, such as washing machines and dishwashers, need a lot of water to work. Until recently, the chemicals in detergents caused pollution to rivers and streams. Today, people are beginning to buy detergents that do not harm the environment.

This Japanese father rinses off all traces of soap from his son's back as he gets into the bath.

For a family bath

In Japan, parents and children often bathe together at home, and friends often meet to relax together in public communal baths. For the Japanese, bathing is not just for getting clean. Usually, bathers wash themselves all over before entering the bath to relax.

This German ad (right), published around 1920, shows a woman dressed for a night out, plugging in her washing machine before she goes.

This kapunuk, a carpet door frame, made by the Tekke Turkmen people of Central Asia, was designed to protect the home from danger and disease.

From danger

Traditionally, many people believed that illness and other misfortunes were caused by evil spirits that brought bad luck. They decorated doorways and windows with special protective patterns, or carved statues of spirits, to guard their buildings and stop any kind of evil entering their homes.

Buddhist palaces and temples in Thailand are protected by huge guardian figures like this giant (right), which stands watchfully in the Grand Palace in Bangkok, Thailand. Built in 1785, it is made of carved and painted wood, with exquisite decoration.

Keeping the home safe

In the past, few countries had police forces to protect people or their homes. Houses were often robbed by criminals, and vandalized by enemy soldiers. Families had to rely on their own strength and skill, and on the strong walls of their homes, for protection. Wealthy nobles built castles, with **moats**, keeps, and towers to keep attackers out. Other people relied on iron bolts, wooden bars, shutters, and fierce guard dogs to keep them safe.

This ancient Greek building is being supported by columns, called Caryatids, carved in the shape of women. The columns bear an enormous weight and keep the building from collapsing.

Locks and keys

Locks stop doors from being opened, except by the person who has the key. The first locks were made almost 6,000 years ago in Ninevah, in the Middle East. They were simple, interlocking pieces of wood, held together by wooden pins. Over the centuries, lock-making grew more complicated, and locksmiths became more skilled.

Holding things up

Ancient buildings had to be well built in order to withstand bad weather, and attacks by enemy invaders. Some ancient Greek buildings are so well designed and made that they are still standing after over 2,000 years.

With moats and towers

Medieval castles built in Europe between around 1050 and 1400 A.D., were large, well-defended houses belonging to kings and powerful noble families. They were also army **barracks**, and centers for running the nobles' great **estates**. Castles were defended by deep moats, strong walls, and look-out towers surrounding a central stronghold, or "keep."

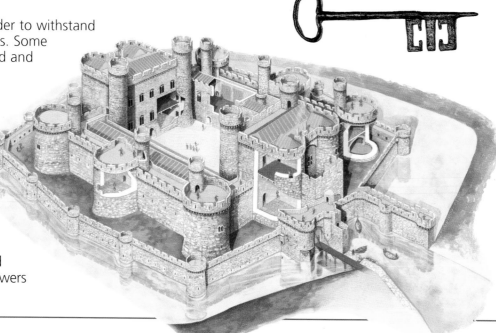

From evil spirits

The Quiang people of Sichuan, China, honor the God of White Stone. They place lumps of sparkling white **quartz** on their roofs and windows, and at each corner of their house, to ask for his protection from evil spirits and illness. They also burn pine branches as an offering to him.

White stones rest above the windows of a Quiang house (above). On the first day of each month the house owner will take some white stones inside, to bring good luck.

Keeping guard dogs

Dogs were one of the first animals to be domesticated, or tamed, by humans around 12,000 years ago. The floor of this house in Pompeii, Italy, dates from almost 2,000 years ago. It is decorated with a mosaic picture of a guard dog. Other homes had a warning in Latin outside their door: *Cave Canem*, or Beware of the Dog!

German Shepherd dogs are one of the most popular breeds used as guard dogs today. Owners say they are intelligent, hard-working, and easily trained.

The household gods

The Romans believed that their homes and families were protected by kind spirits. A Lar was the spirit of the family's ancestors, and spirits called Penates guarded the household's food supplies. A snake-spirit protected the building and its contents.

This lararium, or household shrine, from Pompeii is shaped like a small temple. A genius, or man's guardian spirit, stands in the middle, with two lares, or ancestor spirits, on either side, and a snake spirit below.

Witches keep out!

The traditional homes of the Xhosa people of South Africa were built of woven branches covered with clay, which baked to a hard coating in the hot sun. Each house had a conical thatched roof, one small window, and a strong wooden door. At night, Xhosa families bolted the door and fastened the window securely, to keep evil spirits out.

Can be nuclear

The idea of what makes a family can change through time and across cultures. Families are usually described two ways: the "nuclear" family, which consists of a married couple and their children (left), and the "extended" family that consists of parents, children, grandparents, aunts, uncles, cousins, and relatives by marriage.

This 16th century painting shows King Henri II of France and his wife, Catherine de Medici, surrounded by their extended family.

Families

What is a family? Throughout history, people have given different answers to this question. Families have changed to fit different lifestyles, customs, beliefs, and laws. Families can be very big, with twenty or more relatives living together, or very small, with just one parent and one child. Households can also be big or small, but unlike families, people living in a household do not have to be related. The term household, simply means all the people who live in one home. Wealthy families often have many servants who are not related to them living in their household. Poor families cannot afford servants and their households are often small.

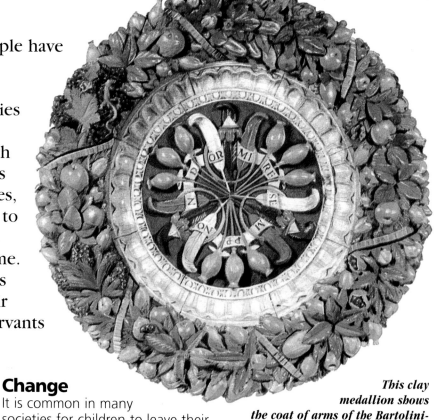

A family from the Trobriand Islands, Papua New Guinea, in traditional clothes. Children there trace their descent through their mother's ancestors, not their father's.

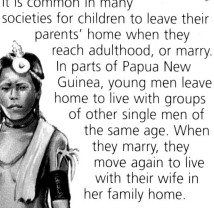

Change

It is common in many societies for children to leave their parents' home when they reach adulthood, or marry. In parts of Papua New Guinea, young men leave home to live with groups of other single men of the same age. When they marry, they move again to live with their wife in her family home.

This clay medallion shows the coat of arms of the Bartolini-Salimbeni family of Florence, Italy. It was made in 1523.

Often have symbols

Many noble families proudly decorated their homes, their clothes, and many other possessions with family symbols, known as "coats of arms." Coats of arms were originally badges designed to be worn on armor in battle and flown on flags. They made it easy for commanders to be recognized by their troops. Coats of arms later became signs of noble rank.

Segregate women and men

Until the 20th century, in most cultures women and men seldom studied or worked side by side. Instead, women and girls spent their lives in quarters separate from the men, where they cooked, made cloth, cared for children, and entertained other women. In some cultures today, houses are still built with separate rooms for women and men. Other homes such as the tents of nomadic Bedouin, and yurts used by people in Central Asia, are divided by a screen or by floor rugs into separate areas for women and men.

This Bedouin mother sits with her child in the women's quarters of her family tent. The Bedouin are nomadic people who live in the deserts of Arabia and North Africa.

One parent

By the late 20th century, many families were headed by just one parent, who lived alone with their children, and had sole responsibility for raising them. In some places, such as North America and Europe, these "single-parent" families resulted from divorce or separation. In other areas, many single parent families began when one partner died from hunger, in wars, or from diseases such as **AIDS**.

Single parents can be mothers or fathers.

Can be extended

Sometimes several generations of a family will share the same rooms in a home, living **communally** and sharing everything. An extended family can mean blood relatives or it can be much more flexible, including relatives by marriage and very good friends.

In some African cultures, such as the Masai in East Africa, a man is allowed to have more than one wife. Often, each of his wives will live separately and have her own house enclosed by a fence. This view seen from a plane shows a village, with cattle protected in the center.

Are home sweet home

All around the world, a home is more than just shelter. It can be a place of welcome, refuge, love, and caring. It can provide people who live there with a sense of comradeship and belonging. It can also give them an identity, and a feeling of self-respect, or family pride. These ideas about homes and families have been described in many poems and songs. They have even been used in ads, such as this poster for new houses in Britain, made around 1930.

Have special meanings

Some buildings are plain and simple. They are shaped liked rectangular blocks, with very little decoration inside or outside. Many other buildings feature roofs, doors, walls, or balconies shaped in beautiful or imaginative ways.

This vase-shaped doorway (left) in a 16th century Chinese walled garden was built to evoke a peaceful feeling. The Chinese word for vase: "ping," sounds the same as the word for "peace."

Special shapes

The architecture of a country or region reflects its history, culture, and environment. The materials available for building also determine the shape and size of structures. It is difficult to build wide rooms or large roofs where there are no tall trees to provide lumber. Sometimes, an oddly shaped site means that a building must be oddly shaped, too. Often, a building's shape is determined by local customs and traditions, or by religious beliefs. Most important of all, a building's shape usually reflects the skills of the people who constructed it, and how it will be used.

The Minangkabau people of Sumatra, Indonesia, build houses with roofs shaped like buffalo horns, a sign of strength and courage. Ancient legends tell how a Minangkabau buffalo once won a great fight against a buffalo from a rival kingdom.

In Yemen

This home in Yemen is built in the shape of a tower, with small windows, which help to keep the house cool by blocking the sunlight. At four stories high, it has **battlements** on the roof, making it difficult for the house to be broken into. It is made of stone and constructed in layers with each floor being used for a different purpose. The ground floor is normally used for storage, the higher floors are usually where the family live, with bedrooms and a kitchen, as well as space to entertain visitors.

In Venice

The city of Venice, Italy, is built around a marshy lagoon. There is very little land suitable for building, so houses are several stories high and tightly packed together, to make the best use of space.

This house in Venice, completed in the 16th century, (left) has been designed with a spiral staircase on the outside of the building, to leave more space in the rooms inside. Spiral stairs take up less space than any other staircase design.

To avoid taxes

Hundreds of new houses (right) were built in the city of Amsterdam, in the Netherlands, between 1550 and 1750. They were tall, and tightly packed together, so that they could be located beside the canals that served the city for roads. The citizens of Amsterdam also had another reason for building tall, narrow houses. Government taxes were calculated according to the width of the canal frontage. The narrower the house, the less tax the owner paid.

For stopping fire

In south-central China, houses were traditionally built with tall, steeped **gables** at each end of their roof. These acted as barriers against fire spreading from one house to another.

The beautiful Chrysler building in New York was designed in the 1920's, in an elegant style called Art Deco which is still popular and much admired today.

Tall gables (above) known as matou qiang, *or "horse's head walls" on traditional Chinese houses. They were made of baked clay bricks covered in plaster, and topped with clay tiles.*

From the past

Many people look back to a "golden age" in their past, when their civilization achieved great things. They admire the buildings and art that were created during that time, and like to decorate modern buildings with designs from history. They restore or make copies of ancient buildings, such as temples or law courts and use them as museums and art galleries.

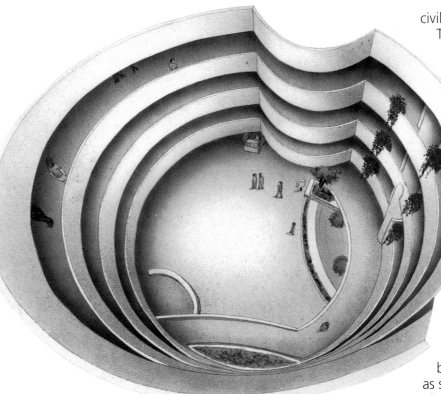

The spiral-shaped Solomon R. Guggenheim Museum in New York was designed by architect Frank Lloyd Wright. Finished in 1959, its special shape gives visitors a clear view of different works of art as they walk down its sloping ramps.

In modern styles

Twentieth-century building technology, such as steel-reinforced concrete, allowed architects to design buildings in new shapes. Instead of just building box-shaped structures, they designed buildings that were curved or even circular.

The Lisu people of southwest China believe that a new home must be built in one day. Taking longer is unlucky. Everyone in the village helps to build the house.

Quickly or slowly

Building a house takes time. The amount of time depends upon the materials used and on the construction techniques. Wooden frames and concrete slabs can be rapidly put together, but it takes much longer to place individual bricks or blocks of stone carefully on top of each other. Planning a new house can also be a slow process. In many countries, local authorities have to be asked for permission before new homes can be built. After that, architects have to draw up plans and discuss them with the home owners.

New homes

Building a new house can be very exciting. In some cultures, new homes are built to satisfy local marriage customs, or to create more space for growing families. In wealthy countries, people build their own homes to suit their lifestyle. They design the house exterior, and arrange the rooms inside exactly the way they want. They can surround their house with strong walls for privacy and security, or with a beautiful garden. For people in poorer parts of the world, building a new house is a matter of necessity. There is less choice about the design of rooms and the materials used in the building. Many traditional homes are made from materials easily damaged by violent storms or floods.

Surrounded by half-built walls and windows, this family in 1960 (above) view the architect's plans for their new home. It can take several months for a brick home to be completed.

Traditionally, among the Drung people of China (below), parents build a new house for each of their sons who gets married. It is located next to their own. Over the years, this creates a row of family houses, side by side.

Keep evil away

In many countries, from North Africa to China, houses are decorated with open hand palm prints to keep evil away. Palm print pictures have also been found in prehistoric caves in Europe and South America. No one knows exactly what they mean.

Can be added

If a family has many children, their home can feel too small. Family businesses, run from home, can also expand and take over living space. Crowded families sometimes move to a new, larger house, or decide to add extra rooms to their existing home, instead.

These men from the village of Shilluk, in the Sudan, are working together to build a new home. Village houses are made of straw tightly bound together to make a frame. They are covered with layers of mud, which bakes hard in the sun.

Use old traditions

There are many ancient traditions associated with building new homes. Sometimes, items such as shoes, coins, or newspapers were buried under the foundations or hidden up chimneys or in walls. People thought these items would bring good luck. A glass ball was hung in the window, to keep witches away. Sometimes, people asked priests to bless a house.

For a new wife

In the Sudan, Africa, a man has to build a new house for his bride to live in, before he can marry her. Other men in his village help him, and the building work becomes part of the wedding celebrations. Many Sudanese people are Muslims, and Muslim law allows a man to have four wives, but only if he can look after them all in the same way! So if a Sudanese man marries several wives, he has to build new houses for all of them.

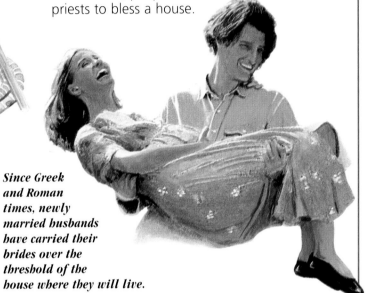

Since Greek and Roman times, newly married husbands have carried their brides over the threshold of the house where they will live.

Many people like to take a small gift with them when they visit friends in a new house for the first time, or when they call on people who have just moved to the neighborhood. Favorite "housewarming" gifts include plants (above) or a bunch of flowers.

Moving into a new home is often an exciting but hectic time, since belongings must be transported from old houses and unpacked in the new home, as this couple (below) are doing. Traditionally, a newly married couple moved into a house together after they were married. It was an important part of starting a new life together.

And moving in

Once a house has been bought or built, it must be prepared so that people can live in it and feel comfortable. This might mean painting the inside, cleaning the house, or arranging the furniture. These things help people to feel relaxed and "at home" in the new **environment**.

From fire

In colder climates, houses need to be heated if the people living there are to survive and feel comfortable in winter. Traditionally, the most common form of heating was an open fire burning in a fireplace. After 1800, free standing stoves made of cast iron (left), were installed in many homes in North America. They were safer, more efficient, and less smoky than open fires.

This large stone fireplace (left) was made for a rich family's house in France around 1450. It is decorated with carvings of wealthy men and women.

Light, heat, and energy

The earliest homes were designed as simple shelters, to protect the people inside from cold, wind, and rain. Over the centuries, house design became more elaborate, with different rooms for different purposes, such as cooking, sleeping, and entertaining visitors. Builders also began to invent ways of keeping houses warm, and lighting them, so that people made more use of their time after dark. Humans found out how to make fire over a million years ago, and the earliest lamps, made to burn animal fat or olive oil, are thousands of years old. By the 1800s, **engineers** found ways of supplying gas and electricity to people's homes.

This tall wood-burning stove (below), covered in brightly-painted tiles, was made in Switzerland in 1600.

From oil lamps to light bulbs

For thousands of years, most people in most parts of the world did not have any easy way of lighting their homes. They relied on the sun for working or for traveling. Their only source of light was firelight or little lamps that burned animal fat called tallow, seal-blubber, or olive oil. Only wealthy people could afford fine beeswax candles, which were made in Europe from the Middle Ages onward. Oil lamps have been in use for thousands of years. The first gas lamps were introduced in Britain in the 1820s, and the first electric light bulbs were made in the U.S. in 1878.

Long-handled copper pans (above), known as warming pans, were filled with burning coals, and used to warm beds before hot water bottles and electric blankets were invented.

Power stations (below) use large magnets moved by turbines as generators to make an electric current. The current flows to a transformer, which increases the voltage, making it easier to transport. The current then flows to the site where it will be used. It passes through a second transformer, to reduce the voltage, ready for use, and flows along underground cables or overhead wires into shops, factories, or people's homes.

Using electricity

Electricity is a natural form of energy that occurs when tiny sub-atomic particles called **electrons** move around. Several different things make electrons move, including **friction**, and thunderstorms. **Batteries** and **generators** make electrons move along wires. This flow is called an electric current. When an electric current flows along the thin wire inside an electric light bulb, it gets so hot that it glows and gives off light.

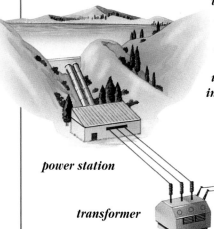

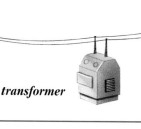
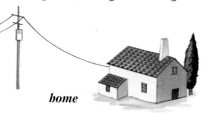

power station

transformer

pylon

transformer

home

To power appliances

By the mid-20th century, most houses in North America and Europe were connected to gas or electricity supplies. Energy for cooking and heating was at the flick of a switch. The first gas or electric stoves, washing machines, and refrigerators were invented in the late 19th century. They were expensive, and many ordinary families could not afford them. As more families became connected to power supplies, and factories introduced mass-production techniques, household appliances became cheaper to buy.

As more women began to work outside the home in industrialized countries, they had less time for household chores. Appliances, like the refrigerator in this advertisement, meant that women, who did most of the household labor, did not have to shop every day for fresh food.

Insulated

Almost all houses are more comfortable to live in if they are well **insulated** from extremes of outside heat or cold. Simple, traditional materials can be used as insulation, such as thick mud walls, or layers of thatch. These act as a barrier, stopping the heat or cold passing through to the inside. The need for insulation has often influenced the place where a house is built. To achieve maximum protection from heat or cold, some houses have even been built underground.

In Greece, summers can be very hot and dry. On many Greek islands and along mainland coasts, there are few trees to provide shade. Houses (below) are often painted bright white on the outside to reflect the heat of the summer sun.

Village homes (left) on the edge of the Sahara Desert, in Natmata, Tunisia, are built underground. The earth insulates them from midday heat and the chill of the desert at night. Each house has rooms arranged around a central courtyard, which is open to the sky, letting in light and fresh air.

From alternative sources

Since the 1960s, engineers in many parts of the world have experimented with new ways of generating electricity to provide energy for heating and lighting homes. Two of their most successful inventions have been domestic windmills, fitted to the roof of this house (right) that harness wind energy, and photovoltaic cells, commonly called "solar panels," that collect energy from the Sun. Solar panels work best in sunny climates and windmills are most useful where strong winds often blow.

This gold-and-silver flambeau, or candle stand (left) was made for French emperor Napoleon in 1809. It has space for eight beeswax candles, and an adjustable shade. Napoleon placed it on his desk, so that he could see to read or write at night.

Must be portable

Nomadic people, who travel from place to place, need homes that are light, simple to dismantle, and easy to move around. This herdsman from the Gaddi people of northwest India has loaded his bedding and furniture on the back of a camel.

For refugees

Charities and international organizations, such as the United Nations, provide tents, blankets, and emergency food and water supplies for **refugees** who have had to flee from their homes. This Bosnian woman and her daughter found shelter in a tent city, along with thousands of other refugees, until it is safe to return to their village.

Homes that change

There is an old saying, "as safe as houses" that is used to describe something that is stable and secure. Today, that saying is no longer true. Many people change their home several times during their lifetime. Some people are nomadic and move frequently to survive. Nomadic peoples need to find fresh food for themselves and their animals. Other people are forced to change their home for work or natural disasters.

Nomadic life

The Hammunat people of Mauritania in northwest Africa are nomadic. They herd sheep and goats in the desert and travel long distances in search of food and water for their animals. Hammunat homes are tents made of woolen cloth stretched over curved wooden poles.

This Romany woman (left), cooking over a campfire, is wearing a headscarf, a traditional sign that she is married. Her husband and son sit close by.

In Hammunat culture, putting up tents and taking them down is traditionally done by women (right).

For gypsies

Originally from north India, the Romany people are sometimes called "gypsies." They live in many countries throughout Europe and North Africa. They move from place to place, working as horse-traders, metal-dealers, and entertainers. Romany families travel with their homes, either traditional covered wagons (above), or modern trailers.

This Kurdish girl (right) is wearing brightly colored traditional clothing. Today, many Kurdish traditions are threatened by the governments of the nations where they live.

Without a homeland

For hundreds of years, the Kurds have made their homes in the Taurus and Zagros mountains, on the borders of Europe and Asia. Today, they have no homeland of their own. The land where they used to live has been divided between Turkey, Iran, Iraq, Syria, and Armenia. Over 17 million Kurds live there. Many do not have proper housing.

A Moken mother and her children (below) shelter from the hot sun under a shady canopy stretched over their boat. At night, they will sleep on the straw mats that are rolled up and neatly stacked away during the day.

On the sea

The Moken people (left) live on boats near the Mergui islands, off the coast of southeast Myanmar. Originally, their homes were on land. According to traditional Moken stories, they began living at sea around 800 A.D. The Moken are said to be the last survivors of the original peoples of Southeast Asia.

The Moken spend most of their time in boats made from hollowed out trees. They come to land only for food, water, or to seek shelter from bad weather.

Because of disasters

Some people lose their homes because of natural disasters. Monsoon rains and tsunamis, or tidal waves, cause devastating floods, and hurricanes and tornadoes rip roofs off buildings. Earthquakes bring houses tumbling to the ground and volcanoes cover nearby villages and farms in lava, ash, and mud.

This Italian family arrived at Ellis Island, the migrants' reception center in New York City, in 1900. They are carrying all their possessions with them.

In 1993 heavy rains caused the Mississippi River in the U.S. to burst its banks. Many people lost their homes in the flood.

Migrants

During the 19th and early 20th centuries, millions of people from Europe and the Middle East migrated to North America. They hoped to find better homes and jobs than the ones they left behind. They also wanted to be free of persecution, on ethnic or religious grounds.

On the streets

There are homeless people all over the world, in rich and poor countries. Some, like beggars who struggle to survive on the streets of cities in India, were born to homeless families. Some, like street children in Africa or South America, are orphans, with no one to care for them. Their parents died from hunger or disease. Many homeless teenagers in Europe and North America have run away from abusive homes. Some older men and women have lost their homes and families, through debt, unemployment, or addiction to drugs. Often, homelessness is not their fault. They live on the streets because they have nowhere else to go.

A homeless person scavenges among garbage bins, hoping to find food. This photo was taken in the 1990s in New York City. Even in the richest country in the world, many people are without permanent homes. They seek warmth and shelter in shopping malls, train stations, underpasses, or in hostels run by city authorities and charities.

Glossary

AIDS: A disease of the immune system that causes infections and cancers. It is transmitted through the bloodstream.

Architect: A person who designs buildings.

Bamboo: The stem of a tall tree-like tropical grass that is used as a building material or for making furniture.

Barrack: A building or group or buildings for lodging people.

Battery: A container which stores and releases electrical energy.

Battlement: A protective railing built on top of a wall of a building for defence.

Bible: A collection of ancient writings that is the sacred book of Christianity.

Cane: A slender, strong, and flexible stem from the bamboo.

Christian: Someone who follows the Christian religion which is based on the life and teachings of Jesus Christ, whom Christians believe is the son of God.

Communally: An activity, such as living or working, done together or in a group.

Communications: A means of sending messages.

Dung: Manure of animals.

Elaborate: To develop or expand in great detail. Elaborate designs are detailed designs.

Electron: A tiny particle inside an atom that contains a small amount of electricity. Everything contains atoms and some electricity.

Embroider: To decorate a piece of cloth by stitching patterns or pictures on to it.

Engineer: A person trained and skilled in the design, construction and use of engines or machines.

Environment: The surroundings or influences under which a person, animal or plant lives or grows.

Estate: A large piece of property or farm. Often, property that is owned by nobles.

Facade: In architecture, the face of a building, especially the decorative face.

Faiths: Beliefs, especially religious ones.

Fax: A method or device for transmitting documents by telephone for exact copies somewhere else.

Friction: The rubbing of the surface on one body against that of another.

Gables: A triangular section of wall at the end of a pitched roof, usually above an arched door or window.

Generation: A period of time marked between the birth of parents and the birth of their children.

Generator: A machine that produces electrical energy. A generator uses magnets and turbines to release electricity and make it flow through wires.

Girders: A horizontal (crosswise) beam used as a main support for a building or bridge.

Geometric: The shape or form of a surface or solid.

Hardwoods: The hard, compact wood or timer of various trees.

Head of State: The head of a country but not necessarily the head of government. For example, the Queen is Britain's head of state but not the head of its government. The president of the United States is both the head of state and head of government.

Hearth: The floor of a fireplace, or the area surrounding a fire.

Insulation: Material that stops heat from escaping a building. Many houses are insulated to stop the cold getting in and the heat getting out.

Lagoon: a shallow body of water, especially one separated from the sea by sandbars or a reef.

Mass produced: Something that is produced in large quantities, especially by machinery in a factory.

Moat: A deep, wide trench, usually filled with water.

Modem: An electronic device used to transmit information on a computer through a telephone wire to another computer.

Mosaic: A picture or design made by setting small pieces of stone, tile, or glass into a surface.

Muslim: A believer in Islam, a religion which follows one God, Allah, and his chief and last prophet, Mohammed.

Palestine: A historical region sometimes called the Holy Land. It is located between the eastern Mediterranean and the Jordan River, (roughly Israel and the West Bank.)

Pasture: Grass or other plants eaten as food by grazing animals such as cows.

Quartz: A hard mineral or crystal used for its ability to create electric signals.

Rafters: A series of timbers that supports the sheathing and covering of a roof.

Refugee: A person forced to leave their country because of persecution, war or natural disasters, such as drought or famine.

Renaissance: A period of European history between the 14th and 16th centuries. A time of great discoveries and development in ideas, writing, music, painting and sculpture.

Reservations: Land set apart for the use of Native American people.

Reservoir: A natural or artificial place where water is collected and stored for use.

Retreat: A place of peace, quiet, and privacy or security.

Romans: A citizen of the ancient Roman Empire which stretched across Europe to Britain and North Africa.

Saints: A person of holiness, who is recognized by the Christian church.

Shrine: A place or structure devoted to a saint, or deity, such as an altar, chapel, or church.

Softwoods: A coniferous tree, or wood that is soft and easily cut.

Textile: Cloth or fabric that has been made by weaving threads together.

Thatch: Plant stalks used as roofing.

Transparent: Something that is clear so that one can see through it, such as a window.

Turbines: A machine where energy is converted to power.

Turf: A layer of grass and sod usually cut from earth.

Voltage: A measure of how hard or powerfully electricity is being pushed through a wire (electric force.)

Index

Acknowledgments

The publishers would like to thank the following picture libraries and photographers for their kind permission to reproduce pictures:

t=top; tl=top left; tc=top center; tr=top right; c=center;

cl=center left; b=bottom; bl=bottom left; bc=bottom center; br=bottom right

Marka: p 9bl; p 30tr
Marco Nardi / McRae Books: p 9br; p 21tr
The Bridgeman Art Library / Overseas: p 13cl; p 17tl; p 22cl; p 26tl
Scala Group, Florence: p 16tl; p 18tl; p 19br; p 21tl; p 26tr
The Stockmarket International / Steve Prezant: p 17br
The Stockmarket International / Tom Stewart: p 17bl
Index / Summerfield: p 18bl
Luciano Pedicini / Archivio dell'Arte: p 19cl
The Stockmarket International / Michael Keller: p 27tr
The Stockmarket International / George Shelley: p 31cl